Icons of America

Megan Kopp and
Heather Kissock

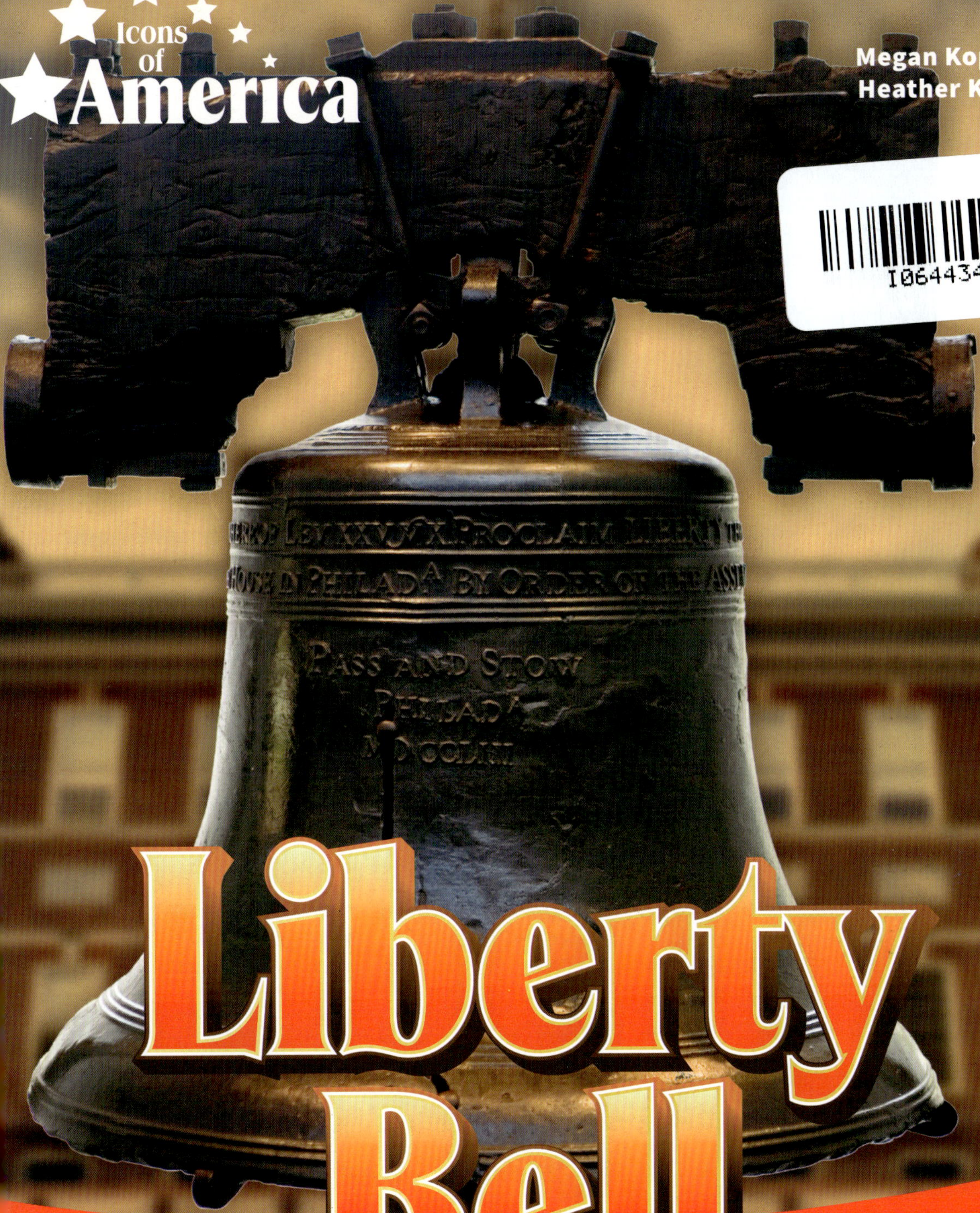

Liberty Bell

AV2
www.av2books.com

Step 1
Go to **www.av2books.com**

Step 2
Enter this unique code

PDTGUHC8N

Step 3
Explore your interactive eBook!

AV2 is optimized for use on any device

Your interactive eBook comes with...

Contents
Browse a live contents page to easily navigate through resources

Audio
Listen to sections of the book read aloud

Videos
Watch informative video clips

Weblinks
Gain additional information for research

Slideshows
View images and captions

Try This!
Complete activities and hands-on experiments

Key Words
Study vocabulary, and complete a matching word activity

Quizzes
Test your knowledge

Share
Share titles within your Learning Management System (LMS) or Library Circulation System

Citation
Create bibliographical references following the Chicago Manual of Style

This title is part of our AV2 digital subscription

1-Year 3–8 Subscription
ISBN 978-1-7911-3306-1

Access hundreds of AV2 titles with our digital subscription.
Sign up for a FREE trial at **www.av2books.com/trial**

Icons of America

Liberty Bell

CONTENTS

A Symbol of Freedom

The Liberty Bell is a symbol of freedom across the United States and around the world. Over the years, the Liberty Bell has been used in ceremonies to represent liberty. It is tapped every year to commemorate the birthday of **civil rights** activist Martin Luther King, Jr. The bell is also an important part of America's Independence Day celebrations.

The bell was made in **London, England**, in **1752**.

A Bell for Pennsylvania

The bell was made to hang from the **steeple** of the Pennsylvania State House, now known as Independence Hall, in Philadelphia.

Independence National Historical Park

Independence Hall and the Liberty Bell are now part of the Independence National Historical Park in Philadelphia, Pennsylvania.

The park was created in 1946.

The park occupies **one** city block called Independence Square.

The park had 4,532,459 visitors in 2019.

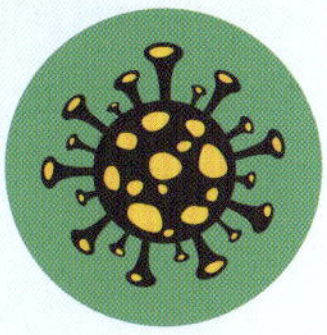

Because of the **COVID-19 pandemic**, park visitors in 2020 dropped to 907,090.

It was used to call politicians to meetings and to gather people for important announcements. It is believed that the bell was **commissioned** to commemorate the 50th anniversary of Pennsylvania's Constitution.

The First Ring

When the bell was delivered, it underwent a test ring. This ring resulted in a crack that rendered the bell useless. The metal was melted down, and the bell was recast. The new bell had an unpleasant tone, so the bell was cast again. This bell was then hung in the State House.

All about the Liberty Bell

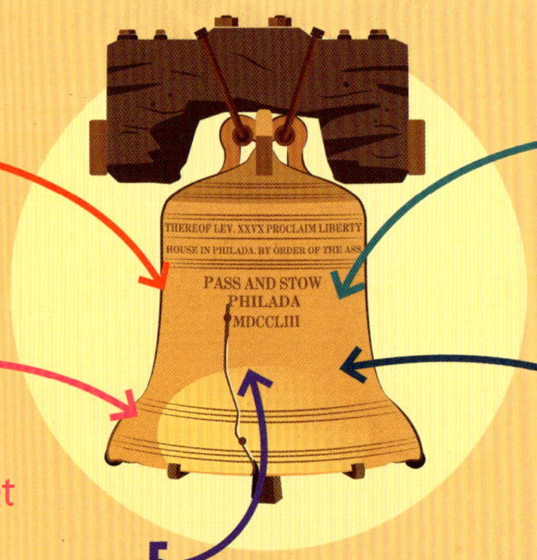

2,080
Weight in pounds (943 kilograms)

70
Percent of the bell made of copper

12
Circumference in feet (3.7 meters)

25
Percent of the bell made of tin

5
Percent of the bell made of other metals, including lead, gold, silver, and zinc

PROCLAIM LIBERTY
BY ORDER OF THE

Words of Freedom

The bell was commissioned by Isaac Norris, the **speaker** of the Pennsylvania Provincial Assembly. He requested that a Bible verse be inscribed on the bell. The verse is from Leviticus 25:10 and reads, “Proclaim liberty throughout all the land unto all the inhabitants thereof.”

Also inscribed on the bell are the names of its creators and its dedication. The state name is spelled "Pensylvania," as there was no official spelling at the time.

Becoming a Symbol

The State House bell was first called the "Liberty Bell" by a group of people trying to abolish slavery. The abolitionists remembered the words on the bell and adopted it as a symbol of their cause. The group used the bell to represent the freedom and independence it sought for all people.

The **United States** officially **abolished slavery** in **1865**.

UNITED STATES
E PLURIBUS UNUM
LIBERTY
IN GOD WE TRUST
1941
1954
OF AMERICA
DOLLAR

A Broken Bell

The bell was used at the Pennsylvania State House until 1846, when it began to crack. The crack was repaired, and the bell was rung on February 23 in honor of George Washington's birthday. Another crack appeared in the bell, rendering it unusable. It has not been rung since, though it is sometimes tapped lightly.

Notable U.S. Bells

The World Peace Bell in Newport, Kentucky, is the largest swinging bell in the United States. It weighs about 33 tons (30 metric tons).

The eight bells of Old North Church in Boston, Massachusetts, are the oldest bells in North America. They were cast in 1744.

The Liberty Bell has more than 50 replicas. The Treasury Department had the replicas made in 1950 and distributed them across the United States.

HOUSE IN PHILADA BY ORDER
PASS AND STOW

A Story of Liberty

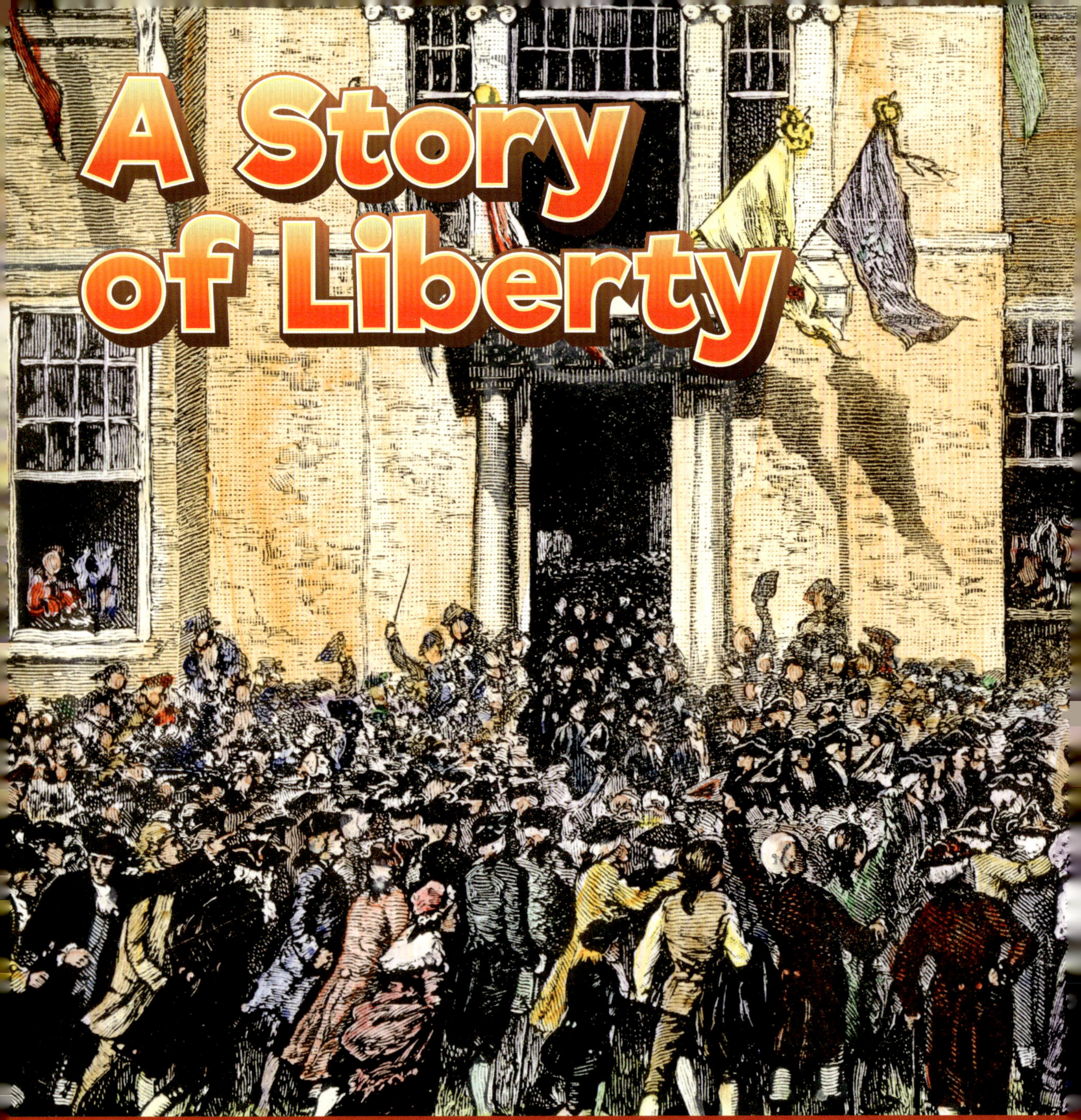

The Liberty Bell became even more of an icon after George Lippard wrote a short story that featured it. The story centered around the ringing of the bell to announce the **Declaration of Independence**.

It is unlikely that this event happened, as the State House steeple was in disrepair by that time. However, the story became part of the country's folklore.

Liberty across America

Starting in the late 1800s, the Liberty Bell began traveling around the country. It was shown at expositions and fairs in an effort to close the rift caused by the Civil War and to remind Americans of their fight for independence from Great Britain.

The Liberty Bell is on **display 24 hours** a day.

RING·HALL·MARVIN SAFE CO

The Liberty Bell Timeline

1751

Commissioning the Bell

The Pennsylvania Provincial Assembly decides to commission a bell for its steeple.

1752

Bell Shipping

The bell is completed. It is transported from London to Philadelphia on a ship called the *Hibernia*.

1753

Testing the Bell

The bell cracks during its test ring. John Pass and John Stow are hired to recast it. Their names appear in the bell's inscription.

1846

Last Ring

The bell is rung for the last time on February 23 to celebrate George Washington's birthday.

1885–1915

Traveling

The bell travels to several cities in the United States, including New Orleans, Chicago, and San Francisco.

2003

Liberty Bell Center

The new Liberty Bell Center opens. One of its walls is made entirely of glass to display the Liberty Bell.

2020

A New Artwork

Liberty Bell, an **augmented reality** artwork created by artist Nancy Baker Cahill, is revealed on July 4. Inspired by the Liberty Bell, it can be seen in six U.S. cities, including Philadelphia.

Liberty Bell Quiz

1 By what name is the Pennsylvania State House known?

2 Who was hired to recast the Liberty Bell in 1753?

3 What happened during the Liberty Bell's test ring?

4 How many Liberty Bell replicas were ordered in 1950?

5 When was Independence National Historical Park created?

6 Who commissioned the Liberty Bell?

7 Where was the Liberty Bell made?

8 Where is the World Peace Bell?

NSWERS

ndependence Hall **2.** John Pass
d John Stow **3.** The bell cracked
More than 50 **5.** 1946 **6.** Isaac Norris,
speaker of the Pennsylvania Provincial
sembly **7.** In London, England
n Newport, Kentucky

Key Words

augmented reality: technology used to add digital information to something being viewed through a device

circumference: the boundary of a circle

civil rights: having equal social opportunties and protection under the law of the country

commissioned: ordered to be made

COVID-19: a viral disease that can cause cough, fever, and trouble breathing, among other symptoms

Declaration of Independence: a document that proclaimed the separation of the American colonies from Great Britain

pandemic: an outbreak of a disease that affects a large percentage of people around the world

speaker: the officer who guides an assembly

steeple: a tall structure situated on top of a building

Index

Published by AV2
276 5th Avenue, Suite 704 #917
New York, NY 10001
Website: www.av2books.com

Library of Congress Cataloging-in-Publication Data

Names: Kopp, Megan, author. | Kissock, Heather, author.
Title: Liberty Bell / Megan Kopp and Heather Kissock.
Description: New York, NY : AV2, [2022] | Series: Icons of America | Includes index. | Audience: Grades 2-3
Identifiers: LCCN 2021003461 (print) | LCCN 2021003462 (ebook) | ISBN 9781791134730 (library binding) | ISBN 9781791134747 (paperback) | ISBN 9781791134754 (ebook other)
Subjects: LCSH: Liberty Bell--Juvenile literature. | Bells--Pennsylvania--Juvenile literature. | Signs and symbols--United States--Juvenile literature. | Liberty--Juvenile literature.
Classification: LCC F158.8.I3 K67 2022 (print) | LCC F158.8.I3 (ebook) | DDC 974.8/11--dc23
LC record available at https://lccn.loc.gov/2021003461
LC ebook record available at https://lccn.loc.gov/2021003462

Printed in Guangzhou, China
1 2 3 4 5 6 7 8 9 0 25 24 23 22 21

042021
101120

Project Coordinator: Sara Cucini
Designer: Jean Faye Marie Rodriguez

Photo Credits
Every reasonable effort has been made to trace ownership and to obtain permission to reprint copyright material. The publisher would be pleased to have any errors or omissions brought to its attention so that they may be corrected in subsequent printings.
AV2 acknowledges Getty Images and Alamy as its primary image suppliers for this title.